M000207067

A gift for

....

From

....

There has not failed
one word of all His
good promise.

1 KINGS 8:56

Praying God's Promises® *for* Your Grandchildren

Illustrations by Sandra Meyer

www.jcountryman.com
A division of Thomas Nelson, Inc.
www.thomasnelson.com

ISBN: 08499-9673-2

www.thomasnelson.com

Printed in Singapore

Contents

Introduction

How precious are our grandchildren. They think we hung the moon—and we know they are each a gifted genius. Grandchildren are treasures to be loved and honored. There are many ways to love and care for them, but one of the most important is to pray for them.

When we pray God's promises, we affirm what He has promised for each child. We agree with His wisdom. We demonstrate our faith and honor Him as our God.

The validity of God's promises rest on His character and His resources. These are revealed to us in the Bible. It tells of His faithfulness, His resources, and His mighty works. Knowing this encourages us to believe that this loving God will also work on behalf of our grandchildren. We can pray God's promises with great confidence!

God's Promises provide guidance and direction so we know how to pray. God has promised that His Word will be a lamp on life's path (Ps. 119:105). It helps us know that we are praying God's will. When you don't know how to pray, ask God to bring particular Scriptures to your mind. He knows the inner needs of your grandchildren. He knows what lies ahead on their particular pathways.

The Word of God will always bring forth fruit. There is power in praying God's Word. The promises of God are dependable: "Not a word failed of any good thing which the LORD has spoken. . . . All came to pass" (Josh. 21:45).

Terri Gibbs,
Editor

How to Pray
God's Promises

Perhaps you are wondering how to pray God's promises. Here is a sample prayer based on Proverbs 3:5–6:

Trust in the LORD with all your heart,
And lean not on your own understanding;
In all your ways acknowledge Him,
And He shall direct your paths.

PRAYER:

Lord, I pray that _____ would trust in you with all his might. I pray that he would not lean on his own knowledge and understanding but that he would acknowledge You and Your guidance. Then I pray, dear Father, that you will make _____ paths straight. Let Your Holy Spirit guide him on those straight paths.

True, whole prayer is
nothing but love.

—ST. AUGUSTINE

LIFE VERSES

Choose a special verse for each grandchild
to pray throughout his or her life.

Life-verse for _____

_____

_____

_____

_____

Life-verse for _____

_____

_____

_____

_____

Life-verse for _____

_____

_____

_____

_____

Life-verse for _____

_____

_____

_____

_____

He prayeth best,

Who loveth best

All things both great and small;

For the dear God

Who loveth us,

He made and loveth all.

SAMUEL TAYLOR COLERIDGE

Prayers for
Daily Needs

"From the time Grandma found out my mother was pregnant, she prayed for me. Every single day. Down through my life, whenever I faced problems, I remembered my grandma praying for me. I knew she wouldn't forget."

JEANNIE ST. JOHN TAYLOR

Confidence

I will praise You, for I am fearfully
and wonderfully made;
Marvelous are Your works,
And that my soul knows very well.

PSALM 139:14

That He would grant you, according to the riches
of His glory, to be strengthened with might
through His Spirit in the inner man.

EPHESIANS 3:16

We are His workmanship, created in Christ Jesus
for good works, which God prepared beforehand
that we should walk in them.

EPHESIANS 2:10

Friends

This is My commandment, that you love one another as I have loved you. Greater love has no one than this, than to lay down one's life for his friends.

JOHN 15:12–13

With all lowliness and gentleness, with longsuffering, bearing with one another in love, endeavoring to keep the unity of the Spirit in the bond of peace.

EPHESIANS 4:2–3

A man who has friends must himself be friendly, but there is a friend who sticks closer than a brother.

PROVERBS 18:24

Prayer is a God-given part
of our urge to protect, care for,
and shape the offspring
He has given us.

DAVID & HEATHER KOPP

Guidance

If any of you lacks wisdom, let him ask of God,
who gives to all liberally and without reproach,
and it will be given to him.

JAMES 1:5

I will instruct you and teach you in the way you
should go; I will guide you with My eye.

PSALM 32:8

Lean not on your own understanding;
in all your ways acknowledge Him and
He shall direct your paths.

PROVERBS 3:6

Health

The LORD will guide you continually,
And satisfy your soul in drought,
And strengthen your bones;
You shall be like a watered garden, and like a
spring of water, whose waters do not fail.

ISAIAH 58:11

Do not be wise in your own eyes; fear the LORD
and depart from evil. It will be health to your
flesh, and strength to your bones.

PROVERBS 3:7–8

I pray that you may prosper in all things and be
in health, just as your soul prospers.

3 JOHN 2

Protection

The LORD, He is the one who goes before you.
He will be with you, He will not leave you nor
forsake you; do not fear nor be dismayed.

DEUTERONOMY 31:8

The LORD will be a shelter for His people,
And the strength of the children of Israel.

JOEL 3:16

When you pass through the waters, I will be with
you; and through the rivers, they shall not overflow
you. When you walk through the fire, you shall
not be burned, nor shall the flame scorch you.

ISAIAH 43:2

Prayers for
Desperate Needs

Anger

Let every man be swift to hear, slow to speak, slow to wrath; for the wrath of man does not produce the righteousness of God.

JAMES 1:19–20

A soft answer turns away wrath, but a harsh word stirs up anger.

PROVERBS 15:1

He who is slow to anger is better than the mighty, and he who rules his spirit than he who takes a city.

PROVERBS 16:32

Anxiety

You will keep him in perfect peace, whose mind
is stayed on You, because he trusts in You.

ISAIAH 26:3

Be anxious for nothing, but in everything by prayer
and supplication, with thanksgiving, let your
requests be made known to God; and the peace of
God, which surpasses all understanding, will guard
your hearts and minds through Christ Jesus.

PHILIPPIANS 4:6–7

May the God of hope fill you with all joy and
peace in believing, that you may abound in hope
by the power of the Holy Spirit.

ROMANS 15:13

Confusion

God is not the author of confusion but of peace,
as in all the churches of the saints.

1 CORINTHIANS 14:33

I was sought by those who did not ask for Me;
I was found by those who did not seek Me.
I said, "Here I am, here I am."

ISAIAH 65:1

I was vexed in my mind. . . .
Nevertheless I am continually with You;
You hold me by my right hand.
You will guide me with Your counsel.

PSALM 73:21–24

God made the sun
And God made the tree,
God made the mountains
And God made me.

LEAH GALE

Depression

Create in me a clean heart, O God,

And renew a steadfast spirit within me.

Do not cast me away from Your presence,

And do not take Your Holy Spirit from me.

Restore to me the joy of Your salvation,

And uphold me by Your generous Spirit.

PSALM 51:10–12

The LORD also will be a refuge for the oppressed,

A refuge in times of trouble.

And those who know Your name will put their

trust in You; for You, LORD, have not forsaken

those who seek You.

PSALM 9:9–10

Discouragement

Who shall separate us from the love of Christ?
Shall tribulation, or distress, or persecution,
or famine, or nakedness, or peril, or sword? . . .
Yet in all these things we are more than
conquerors through Him who loved us.

ROMANS 8:35–37

Turn Yourself to me, and have mercy on me,
For I am desolate and afflicted.
The troubles of my heart have enlarged;
Bring me out of my distresses! . . .
Keep my soul and deliver me;
Let me not be ashamed, for I put my trust in You.

PSALM 25:15–20

Failure

I, the LORD your God, will hold your right hand,
Saying to you, "Fear not, I will help you."

ISAIAH 41:13

Now may our Lord Jesus Christ Himself, and
our God and Father, who has loved us and given
us everlasting consolation and good hope by
grace, comfort your hearts and establish you
in every good word and work.

2 THESSALONIANS 2:16–17

I will lead them in paths they have not known.
I will make darkness light before them, and
crooked places straight. These things I will do
for them, and not forsake them.

ISAIAH 42:16

Fear

The LORD is my light and my salvation;
Whom shall I fear?
The LORD is the strength of my life;
Of whom shall I be afraid?

PSALM 27:1

There is no fear in love; but perfect love casts out
fear, because fear involves torment. But he who
fears has not been made perfect in love.

1 JOHN 4:18

The LORD is my strength and my shield;
My heart trusted in Him, and I am helped;
Therefore my heart greatly rejoices,
And with my song I will praise Him.

PSALM 28:7

*Prayer is
an invitation to God to
intervene in our lives,
to let His will
prevail in our affairs.*

ABRAHAM HESCHEL

Grief

He is despised and rejected by men,

A Man of sorrows and acquainted with grief.

And we hid, as it were, our faces from Him;

He was despised, and we did not esteem Him.

ISAIAH 53:3

You have seen, for You observe trouble and grief,

To repay it by Your hand.

The helpless commits himself to You;

You are the helper of the fatherless.

PSALM 10:14

The LORD has anointed me . . . to comfort all

who mourn, . . . to give them beauty for ashes,

the oil of joy for mourning.

ISAIAH 61:1–2

Heartbreak

Those who sow in tears shall reap in joy.
He who continually goes forth weeping, bearing
seed for sowing, shall doubtless come again with
rejoicing, bringing his sheaves with him.

PSALM 126:5–6

Cast your burden on the LORD, and He
shall sustain you; He shall never permit the
righteous to be moved.

PSALM 55:22

The LORD has anointed Me, to preach
good tidings to the poor; He has sent
Me to heal the brokenhearted.

ISAIAH 61:1

Hopelessness

Why are you cast down, O my soul?
And why are you disquieted within me?
Hope in God; for I shall yet praise Him,
The help of my countenance and my God.

PSALM 42:11

I will be glad and rejoice in Your mercy,
For You have considered my trouble;
You have known my soul in adversities,

PSALM 31:7

The LORD is good, a stronghold
in the day of trouble; and He knows
those who trust in Him.

NAHUM 1:7

God be in my head
and in my understanding.
God be in mine eyes
and in my looking.
God be in my mouth
and in my speaking.
God by in my heart
and in my thinking.

ANONYMOUS

Insecurities

He gives power to the weak,
And to those who have no might
He increases strength.

ISAIAH 40:29

In returning and rest you shall be saved;
In quietness and confidence
shall be your strength.

ISAIAH 30:15

But those who wait on the LORD
Shall renew their strength;
They shall mount up with wings like eagles,
They shall run and not be weary,
They shall walk and not faint.

ISAIAH 40:31

Loneliness

Be strong and of good courage, do not fear nor
be afraid of them; for the LORD your God, He is
the One who goes with you. He will not leave
you nor forsake you.

DEUTERONOMY 31:6

He who dwells in the secret place
of the Most High shall abide under the
shadow of the Almighty.

PSALM 91:1

The LORD is near to all who call upon Him,
To all who call upon Him in truth.
He will fulfill the desire of those who fear Him;
He also will hear their cry and save them.

PSALM 145:18–19

Nightmares

I will both lie down in peace, and sleep;
For You alone, O LORD, make me dwell in safety.

PSALM 4:8

Peace I leave with you, My peace I give to you; not
as the world gives do I give to you. Let not your
heart be troubled, neither let it be afraid.

JOHN 14:27

For God has not given us a spirit of fear,
but of power and of love and of a sound mind.

2 TIMOTHY 1:7

Obsessions

Save me, O God, by Your name, and vindicate me
by Your strength. Hear my prayer, O God;
Give ear to the words of my mouth. For strangers
have risen up against me, and oppressors have
sought after my life.

PSALM 54:1–3

Give us help from trouble, for the help of man
is useless. Through God we will do valiantly,
for it is He who shall tread down our enemies.

PSALM 60:11–12

The Lord God is my strength; He will make
my feet like deer's feet, and He will make me walk
on my high hills.

HABAKKUK 3:19

Rebellion

See, O LORD, that I am in distress;
My soul is troubled;
My heart is overturned within me,
For I have been very rebellious.
Outside the sword bereaves,
At home it is like death.

LAMENTATIONS 1:20

Open their eyes, in order to turn them from
darkness to light, and from the power of Satan
to God, that they may receive forgiveness of sins
and an inheritance among those who are
sanctified by faith in Me.

ACTS 26:18

Grace is love that
cares and stoops and rescues.

———

JOHN STOTT

Rejection

But I say to you who hear: Love your enemies,
do good to those who hate you, bless those
who curse you, and pray for those who
spitefully use you.

LUKE 6:27–28

The LORD also will be a refuge for the oppressed,
a refuge in times of trouble.

PSALM 9:9

The LORD God will help Me;
Therefore I will not be disgraced;
Therefore I have set My face like a flint,
And I know that I will not be ashamed.

ISAIAH 50:7

Sadness

The ransomed of the LORD shall return,
and come to Zion with singing,
with everlasting joy on their heads. They shall
obtain joy and gladness, and sorrow and
sighing shall flee away.

ISAIAH 35:10

My soul shall be satisfied as with marrow
and fatness, and my mouth shall praise You with
joyful lips. When I remember You on my bed,
I meditate on You in the night watches.
Because You have been my help, therefore in
the shadow of Your wings I will rejoice.

PSALM 63:5–7

Sickness

Bless the LORD, O my soul, and forget not all
His benefits: Who forgives all your iniquities,
Who heals all your diseases.

PSALM 103:2–3

Who Himself bore our sins in His own
body on the tree, that we, having died to sins,
might live for righteousness—by whose
stripes you were healed.

1 PETER 2:24

Therefore we do not lose heart. Even though
our outward man is perishing, yet the inward
man is being renewed day by day.

2 CORINTHIANS 4:16

Keep praying,
but be thankful that God's answers
are wiser than your prayers!

WILLIAM CULBERTSON

Prayers for Deliverance

Addictive Behavior

Now the Lord is the Spirit; and where the
Spirit of the Lord is, there is liberty.

2 CORINTHIANS 3:17

And you shall know the truth, and the truth
shall make you free. Therefore if the Son makes
you free, you shall be free indeed.

JOHN 8:32, 36

He has redeemed my soul in peace from
the battle that was against me, for there
were many against me.

PSALM 55:18

Therefore submit to God. Resist the devil
and he will flee from you.

JAMES 4:7

False Doctrine

Whatever things are true, whatever things are noble, whatever things are just, whatever things are pure, whatever things are lovely, whatever things are of good report, if there is any virtue and if there is anything praiseworthy—meditate on these things.

PHILIPPIANS 4:8

Beware of false prophets, who come to you in sheep's clothing, but inwardly they are ravenous wolves. You will know them by their fruits. Do men gather grapes from thorn bushes or figs from thistles? Even so, every good tree bears good fruit, but a bad tree bears bad fruit.

MATTHEW 7:15–17

Peer Pressure

Now to Him who is able to keep you from stumbling, and to present you faultless before the presence of His glory with exceeding joy, to God our Savior, who alone is wise, be glory and majesty, dominion and power, both now and forever.

JUDE 24, 25

Keep your heart with all diligence, for out of it spring the issues of life. . . . Let your eyes look straight ahead, and your eyelids look right before you. Ponder the path of your feet, and let all your ways be established. Do not turn to the right or the left; remove your foot from evil.

PROVERBS 4:23–27

May those who come
behind us find us faithful.

JOHN MOHR

Temptation

The Lord knows how to deliver the godly out
of temptations and to reserve the unjust under
punishment for the day of judgment.

2 PETER 2:9

Blessed is the man who endures temptation;
for when he has been approved, he will receive
the crown of life.

JAMES 1:12

No temptation has overtaken you except such as
is common to man; but God is faithful, who will
not allow you to be tempted beyond what you are
able, but with the temptation will also make the
way of escape, that you may be able to bear it.

1 CORINTHIANS 10:13

Traumas

Before I formed you in the womb I knew you.

JEREMIAH 1:5

In righteousness you shall be established;
you shall be far from oppression,
for you shall not fear; and from terror,
for it shall not come near you.

ISAIAH 54:14

You have also given me the shield of
Your salvation; Your right hand has held me up,
Your gentleness has made me great.
You enlarged my path under me,
So my feet did not slip.

PSALM 18:35–36

No child should ever miss
the privilege of being a grandchild.
Grandchildren get preferred status.

BRUCE AND STAN

Prayers for
Protection

Danger

He will gather the lambs with His arms,
and carry them in His bosom.

ISAIAH 40:11

The LORD will be a shelter for His people,
and the strength of the children of Israel.

JOEL 3:16

Yea, though I walk through the valley of the
shadow of death,
I will fear no evil;
For You are with me;
Your rod and Your staff, they comfort me.

PSALM 23:4

Demonic Forces

He has delivered us from the power of
darkness and conveyed us into the kingdom
of the Son of His love.

COLOSSIANS 1:13

No weapon formed against you shall prosper,
and every tongue which rises against
you in judgment.

ISAIAH 54:17

The Lord will deliver me from every evil work
and preserve me for His heavenly kingdom.
To Him be glory forever and ever.

2 TIMOTHY 4:18

*Those things we see as
impossible mountains in the lives
of our [grand]children can be
removed by praying the promises
of Scripture—God's Word.*

FERN NICHOLS

Sexual Impurity

Walk in the Spirit, and you shall not fulfill
the lust of the flesh.

GALATIANS 5:16

He who commits sexual immorality
sins against his own body.
Do you not know that your body
is the temple of the Holy Spirit
who is in you?

1 CORINTHIANS 6:18–19

How can a young man cleanse his way?
By taking heed according to Your word.

PSALM 119:9

Worldly Influences

Do not imitate what is evil, but what is good.
He who does good is of God.

3 JOHN 11

Be strong and of good courage; do not be afraid,
nor be dismayed, for the LORD your God
is with you wherever you go.

JOSHUA 1:9

Those who trust in the LORD
Are like Mount Zion,
Which cannot be moved, but abides forever.
Do good, O LORD, to those who are good,
And to those who are upright in their hearts.

PSALM 125:1, 4

When you think about it,
the opportunity to pray is an
amazing invitation from the One who
loves us most. Almost as hard to resist
as a puddle full of stars.

DAVID & HEATHER KOPP

Praying for your
[grand]children's salvation
is asking God to give them the
only gift that lasts forever.

———

JODIE BERNDT

Prayers for Spiritual
Development

Accept Salvation

If you confess with your mouth the Lord Jesus
and believe in your heart that God has raised
Him from the dead, you will be saved. For with
the heart one believes unto righteousness, and
with the mouth confession is made unto salvation.

ROMANS 10:9–10

Behold, I stand at the door and knock. If anyone
hears My voice and opens the door, I will come in
to him and dine with him, and he with Me.

REVELATION 3:20

In Him we have redemption
through His blood.

EPHESIANS 1:7

Become Disciples

Let us not grow weary while doing good, for in
due season we shall reap if we do not lose heart.

GALATIANS 6:9

If anyone desires to come after Me, let him deny
himself, and take up his cross daily, and follow Me.
For whoever desires to save his life will lose it, but
whoever loses his life for My sake will save it.

LUKE 9:23–24

If we endure, we shall also reign with Him.
If we deny Him, He also will deny us.
If we are faithless, He remains faithful;
He cannot deny Himself.

2 TIMOTHY 2:11–13

It is God's will
to hear prayer and to do
what faith in His Word
desires and accepts.

ANDREW MURRAY

Know Righteousness

Keep justice, and do righteousness,

For My salvation is about to come,

And My righteousness to be revealed.

Blessed is the man who does this.

ISAIAH 56:1

The LORD will give what is good; . . .

Righteousness will go before Him,

And shall make His footsteps our pathway.

PSALM 85:12–13

When He, the Spirit of truth, has come,

He will guide you into all truth; for He will not

speak on His own authority, but whatever

He hears He will speak.

JOHN 16:13

Know Truth

Through Your precepts I get understanding;
Therefore I hate every false way.

PSALM 119:104

Let the word of Christ dwell in you richly in all
wisdom, teaching and admonishing one another
in psalms and hymns and spiritual songs, singing
with grace in your hearts to the Lord.

COLOSSIANS 3:16

But he who looks into the perfect law of liberty
and continues in it, and is not a forgetful hearer
but a doer of the word, this one will be blessed
in what he does.

JAMES 1:25

Obey God

My son, do not forget my law,

But let your heart keep my commands;

For length of days and long life

And peace they will add to you.

PROVERBS 3:1–2

Great peace have those who love Your law,

and nothing causes them to stumble.

PSALM 119:165

I can do all things through Christ

who strengthens me.

PHILIPPIANS 4:13

Serve God

How beautiful upon the mountains
Are the feet of him who brings good news,
Who proclaims peace, who brings glad tidings
of good things, who proclaims salvation,
Who says to Zion, "Your God reigns!"

ISAIAH 52:7

If anyone is in Christ, he is a new creation;
old things have passed away; behold, all things
have become new.

2 CORINTHIANS 5:17

I am the vine, you are the branches. He who
abides in Me, and I in him, bears much fruit;
for without Me you can do nothing.

JOHN 15:5

Dear Father,
Hear and bless
Thy beasts and singing birds.
And guard with tenderness
Small things that have no words.

ANONYMOUS

Stand Strong

We also glory in tribulations, knowing that
tribulation produces perseverance; and
perseverance, character; and character, hope.

ROMANS 5:3–5

You have need of endurance, so that
after you have done the will of God,
you may receive the promise.

HEBREWS 10:36

Be steadfast, immovable, always abounding in the
work of the Lord, knowing that your labor is not
in vain in the Lord.

1 CORINTHIANS 15:58

Turn Back to God

I have loved you with an everlasting love;
Therefore with lovingkindness I have drawn you.

JEREMIAH 31:3

Return, you backsliding children,
And I will heal your backslidings.

JEREMIAH 3:22

Let the wicked forsake his way,
And the unrighteous man his thoughts;
Let him return to the LORD,
And He will have mercy on him;
And to our God, for He will abundantly pardon.

ISAIAH 55:7

Use Talents Wisely

If anyone cleanses himself . . . , he will be
a vessel for honor, sanctified and useful for the
Master, prepared for every good work.

2 TIMOTHY 2:21

He who believes in Me, as the Scripture has said,
out of his heart will flow rivers of living water.s

JOHN 7:38

As each one has received a gift,
minister it to one another, as good stewards
of the manifold grace of God.

1 PETER 4:10

Prayers for
Christ-Like Character

Compassion

All of you be of one mind,

having compassion for one another;

love as brothers, be tenderhearted, be courteous.

1 PETER 3:8

He who finds his life will lose it,

and he who loses his life for My sake

will find it.

MATTHEW 10:39

He who has pity on the poor lends to the LORD,

and He will pay back what he has given.

PROVERBS 19:17

Commitment

Whatever you do, do it heartily, as to the Lord and
not to men, knowing that from the Lord
you will receive the reward of the inheritance;
for you serve the Lord Christ.

COLOSSIANS 3:23–24

Being confident of this very thing, that He
who has begun a good work in you will complete
it until the day of Jesus Christ.

PHILIPPIANS 1:6

Let us not grow weary while doing good, for in
due season we shall reap if we do not lose heart.

GALATIANS 6:9

Contentment

We know that all things work together for good
to those who love God, to those who are the
called according to His purpose.

ROMANS 8:28

Let your conduct be without covetousness;
be content with such things as you have. For He
Himself has said, "I will never leave you nor forsake
you." So we may boldly say: "The Lord is my
helper; I will not fear. What can man do to me?"

HEBREWS 13:5–6

Delight yourself also in the LORD, and He shall
give you the desires of your heart.

PSALM 37:4

Courage

Wait on the LORD be of good courage,
And He shall strengthen your heart;
Wait, I say, on the LORD!

PSALM 27:14

Be strong and of good courage, do not fear nor
be afraid of them; for the LORD your God,
He is the One who goes with you. He will not
leave you nor forsake you.

DEUTERONOMY 31:6

Have I not commanded you?
Be strong and of good courage; do not be afraid,
nor be dismayed, for the LORD your God
is with you wherever you go.

JOSHUA 1:9

God is all love,
and those who trust Him
need never know anything
but that love.

A. W. TOZER

Endurance

Blessed is the man who endures temptation;
for when he has been approved, he will receive
the crown of life which the Lord has promised
to those who love Him.

JAMES 1:12

But He knows the way that I take;
When He has tested me,
I shall come forth as gold.

JOB 23:10

If anyone serves Me, let him follow Me;
and where I am, there My servant will be also.
If anyone serves Me, him My Father will honor.

JOHN 12:26

Forgiveness

Let all bitterness, wrath, anger, clamor,
and evil speaking be put away from you,
with all malice. And be kind to one another,
tenderhearted, forgiving one another, just as
God in Christ forgave you.

EPHESIANS 4:31–32

If you forgive men their trespasses, your heavenly
Father will also forgive you.

MATTHEW 6:14

Judge not, and you shall not be judged.
Condemn not, and you shall not be condemned.
Forgive, and you will be forgiven.

LUKE 6:37

Honesty

He who speaks truth declares righteousness,
but a false witness, deceit. The truthful lip shall be
established forever, but a lying tongue
is but for a moment.

PROVERBS 12:17,19

In mercy and truth atonement
is provided for iniquity; and by the fear of
the LORD one departs from evil.

PROVERBS 16:6

Let no corrupt word proceed out of your mouth,
but what is good for necessary edification,
that it may impart grace to the hearers.

EPHESIANS 4:29

Humility

I will praise the name of God with a song,
and will magnify Him with thanksgiving.
This also shall please the Lord better than
an ox or bull, which has horns and hooves.
The humble shall see this and be glad;
And you who seek God, your hearts shall live.

PSALM 69:30–32

Who is wise and understanding among you?
Let him show by good conduct that his works
are done in the meekness of wisdom.

JAMES 3:13

Whoever humbles himself as this little child is
the greatest in the kingdom of heaven.

MATTHEW 18:4

Kindness

Give, and it will be given to you: good measure,
pressed down, shaken together, and running over
will be put into your bosom. For with the same
measure you use, it will be measured back to you.

LUKE 6:38

Honor the LORD with your possessions,
And with the firstfruits of all your increase;
So your barns will be filled with plenty,
And your vats will overflow with new wine.

PROVERBS 3:9–10

Love suffers long and is kind.

1 CORINTHIANS 13:4

Let us pray, for God loves us.
Let us pray, for God hears us.
Let us pray, for God is our God,
and we are all His children.

ANONYMOUS

Love

Therefore be imitators of God as dear children.
And walk in love, as Christ also has loved us and
given Himself for us, an offering and a sacrifice
to God for a sweet-smelling aroma.

EPHESIANS 5:1–2

Above all these things put on love, which is
the bond of perfection.

COLOSSIANS 3:14

Let love be without hypocrisy. Abhor what is evil.
Cling to what is good. Be kindly affectionate to
one another with brotherly love, in honor giving
preference to one another.

ROMANS 12:9–10

Obedience

A wise son heeds his father's instruction,
but a scoffer does not listen to rebuke.

PROVERBS 13:1

I will instruct you and teach you
in the way you should go;
I will guide you with My eye.

PSALM 32:8

Honor your father and your mother,
that your days may be long upon the land
which the LORD your God is giving you.

EXODUS 20:12

Patience

Therefore be patient, brethren, until the coming
of the Lord. See how the farmer waits for the
precious fruit of the earth, waiting patiently for
it until it receives the early and latter rain.
You also be patient. Establish your hearts,
for the coming of the Lord is at hand.

JAMES 5:7–8

Now no chastening seems to be joyful for the
present, but painful; nevertheless, afterward it
yields the peaceable fruit of righteousness to
those who have been trained by it.

HEBREWS 12:11

Purity

No fornicator, unclean person,
nor covetous man, who is an idolater, has any
inheritance in the kingdom of Christ and God.
Let no one deceive you with empty words,
for because of these things the wrath of God
comes upon the sons of disobedience.

EPHESIANS 5:5–7

I say then: Walk in the Spirit, and you shall not
fulfill the lust of the flesh.

GALATIANS 5:16

He who walks with integrity walks securely.

PROVERBS 10:9

Wisdom

I will give you a mouth and wisdom
which all your adversaries will not be able
to contradict or resist.

LUKE 21:15

I have taught you in the way of wisdom;
I have led you in right paths.
When you walk, your steps will not be hindered,
And when you run, you will not stumble.
Take firm hold of instruction, do not let go;
Keep her, for she is your life.

PROVERBS 4:11–13

If any of you lacks wisdom, let him ask of God,
who gives to all liberally and without reproach,
and it will be given to him.

JAMES 1:5

*Spread out your
petition before God, and then say,
"Thy will, not mine, be done."*

DWIGHT L. MOODY

Prayers for
God's Blessings

Abundant Good

The LORD God is a sun and shield;
The LORD will give grace and glory;
No good thing will He withhold
From those who walk uprightly.

PSALM 84:11

He will bless those who fear the LORD,
Both small and great.

PSALM 115:13

God is able to make all grace abound
toward you, that you, always having all
sufficiency in all things, may have an
abundance for every good work.

2 CORINTHIANS 9:8

Divine Intervention

The angel of the LORD encamps all around
those who fear Him, and delivers them.

PSALM 34:7

I have put My words in your mouth;
I have covered you with the shadow of My hand.

ISAIAH 51:16

By You I have been upheld from birth;
You are He who took me out of my
   mother's womb.
My praise shall be continually of You.

PSALM 71:6

Gifts

There are diversities of gifts, but the
same Spirit. There are differences of ministries,
but the same Lord.

1 CORINTHIANS 12:4,5

As each one has received a gift,
minister it to one another, as good stewards
of the manifold grace of God.

1 PETER 4:10

Every good gift and every perfect gift is
from above, and comes down from the Father
of lights, with whom there is no variation
or shadow of turning.

JAMES 1:17

Prayer is the way into God,
the way into knowing His heart,
the way into abiding in His love.
It is also the way out of…
anxiety, burdens, and all
that causes heaviness.

RUTH BELL GRAHAM

Grace

The LORD God is a sun and shield;
The LORD will give grace and glory;
No good thing will He withhold
From those who walk uprightly.

PSALM 84:11

He has not dealt with us according to our sins,
Nor punished us according to our iniquities.
For as the heavens are high above the earth,
So great is His mercy toward those who fear Him;

PSALM 103:10–11

Joy

The righteous shall be glad in the LORD,
and trust in Him.
And all the upright in heart shall glory.

PSALM 64:10

Then our mouth was filled with laughter,
And our tongue with singing. Then they said
among the nations, "the LORD has done great
things for them." The LORD has done great things
for us, and we are glad.

PSALM 126:2–3

These things I have spoken to you, that My joy
may remain in you, and that your joy may be full.

JOHN 15:11

Peace

The LORD will give strength to His people;
The LORD will bless His people with peace.

PSALM 29:11

For you shall go out with joy,
And be led out with peace;
The mountains and the hills
Shall break forth into singing before you,
And all the trees of the field shall clap their hands.

ISAIAH 55:12

Peace I leave with you, My peace I give to you;
not as the world gives do I give to you. Let not
your heart be troubled, neither let it be afraid.

JOHN 14:27

*Children wrap themselves
around our hearts, and when we see
their pain we are full of anguish.*

C. H. SPURGEON

Every child has been
created for greater things,
to love and be loved,
in the image of God.

MOTHER TERESA

General Promises for
Your Grandchildren

God Is Faithful

He Himself has said,
"I will never leave you nor forsake you."

HEBREWS 13:5

Lo, I am with you always,
even to the end of the age.

MATTHEW 28:20

His compassions fail not,
They are new every morning;
Great is Your faithfulness.

LAMENTATIONS 3:22–23

God Is Love

But God demonstrates His own love toward us, in that while we were still sinners, Christ died for us.

ROMANS 5:8

We love Him because He first loved us.

1 JOHN 4:19

We have known and believed the love that God has for us. God is love, and he who abides in love abides in God, and God in him.

1 JOHN 4:16

God Is Their Father

"I will be a Father to you,
and you shall be My sons and daughters,"
says the LORD Almighty.

2 CORINTHIANS 6:18

As a father pities his children,
So the LORD pities those who fear Him.

PSALM 103:13

You, O LORD, are our Father;
Our Redeemer from Everlasting is Your name.

ISAIAH 63:16

May the love of God our Father
Be in all our homes today;
May the love of the Lord Jesus
Keep our hearts and minds always.

ANONYMOUS

God Is Their Guide

This is God,

Our God forever and ever;

He will be our guide

Even to death.

PSALM 48:14

When He, the Spirit of truth, has come,

He will guide you into all truth.

JOHN 16:13

The LORD is my shepherd;

I shall not want.

He makes me to lie down in green pastures;

He leads me beside the still waters.

PSALM 23:1–2

God—Their Provider

My God shall supply all your need according
to His riches in glory by Christ Jesus.

PHILIPPIANS 4:19

You are the God who does wonders; You have
declared Your strength among the peoples.

PSALM 77:14

The Lord your God is He who goes with you,
to fight for you against your enemies, to save you.

DEUTERONOMY 20:4

He will deliver the needy when he cries,
The poor also, and him who has no helper.

PSALM 72:12

God's Plan

All that the Father gives Me will come to Me,
and the one who comes to Me I will
by no means cast out.

JOHN 6:37

I know the thoughts that I think toward you,
says the LORD, thoughts of peace and not of evil,
to give you a future and a hope.

JEREMIAH 29:11

Being confident of this very thing,
that He who has begun a good work in you
will complete it until the day of Jesus Christ.

PHILIPPIANS 1:6

Heaven—Their Home

This is the will of Him who sent Me,
that everyone who sees the Son and believes
in Him may have everlasting life; and I will
raise him up at the last day.

JOHN 6:40

The hope which is laid up for you in heaven,
of which you heard before in the word of the
truth of the gospel, which has come to you.

COLOSSIANS 1:5–6

Our citizenship is in heaven, from which we also
eagerly wait for the Savior, the Lord Jesus Christ.

PHILIPPIANS 3:20

Jesus—Their Savior

It is not the will of your Father who is in heaven
that one of these little ones should perish.

MATTHEW 18:14

Believe on the Lord Jesus Christ, and you will
be saved, you and your household.

ACTS 16:31

Whoever calls on the name
of the Lord shall be saved.

ROMANS 10:13

Whoever confesses that Jesus is the Son of God,
God abides in him, and he in God.

1 JOHN 4:15

To children . . .
give always a happy smile.
Give them not only your care,
but also your heart.

MOTHER TERESA

God reached into my life
when I was merely a tiny embryo
and began to shape me within. He began
to put me together while I was still in
the soft silence of my mother's womb.

CHARLES R. SWINDOLL

Prayers of Praise and Thanksgiving

Answered Prayer

It shall come to pass that before they call,
I will answer; and while they are still speaking,
I will hear.

ISAIAH 65:24

Oh, sing to the LORD a new song! For He has
done marvelous things; His right hand and His
holy arm have gained Him the victory.

PSALM 98:1

Your Father knows the things
you have need of before you ask Him.

MATTHEW 6:8

God's Goodness

Be thankful to Him, and bless His name.
For the LORD is good;
His mercy is everlasting,
And His truth endures to all generations.

PSALM 100:4–5

To Him who is able to do exceedingly abundantly
above all that we ask or think, according to the
power that works in us, to Him be glory . . .
forever and ever.

EPHESIANS 3:20–21

I would have lost heart, unless I had believed
that I would see the goodness of the LORD
in the land of the living.

PSALM 27:13

No life of faith can
be lived privately. There must be
overflow into the lives of others.

EUGENE H. PETERSON

Praise to God

Let us continually offer the sacrifice of praise
to God, that is, the fruit of our lips,
giving thanks to His name.

HEBREWS 13:15

As for God, His way is perfect;
The word of the LORD is proven;
He is a shield to all who trust in Him.

PSALM 18:30

He is your praise, and He is your God,
who has done for you these great and awesome
things which your eyes have seen.

DEUTERONOMY 10:21

Thanks for All Things

My God shall supply all your need according
to His riches in glory by Christ Jesus.

PHILIPPIANS 4:19

I will sing to the LORD as long as I live;
I will sing praise to my God while I have
my being.

PSALM 104:33

In everything give thanks; for this is
the will of God in Christ Jesus for you.

1 THESSALONIANS 5:18

Promises About

Prayer

He who promised is faithful.

HEBREWS 10:23

O LORD God, You are God,
and Your words are true.

2 SAMUEL 7:28

This is the confidence that we have in Him,
that if we ask anything according to His will,
He hears us. And if we know that He hears us,
whatever we ask, we know that we have the
petitions that we have asked of Him.

1 JOHN 5:14–15

The eyes of the Lord are on the righteous,
and His ears are open to their prayers.

1 PETER 3:12

Confess your trespasses to one another,
and pray for one another, that you may be healed.
The effective, fervent prayer of a righteous
man avails much.

JAMES 5:16

Whatever you ask the Father in My name He
will give you. Until now you have asked nothing
in My name. Ask, and you will receive, that your
joy may be full.

JOHN 16:23, 24

Whatever you bind on earth will be bound
in heaven, and whatever you loose on earth
will be loosed in heaven.

MATTHEW 18:18

It shall come to pass
That before they call, I will answer;
And while they are still speaking, I will hear.

ISAIAH 65:24

Then you will call upon Me and go and pray
to Me, and I will listen to you.

JEREMIAH 29:12

Let us therefore come boldly to the throne
of grace, that we may obtain mercy and find
grace to help in time of need.

HEBREWS 4:16

If you can believe, all things are possible
to him who believes.

MARK 9:2

Personal Promises for
Your Grandchildren

Personal promises to pray for your grandchildren:

_____

_____

_____

_____

_____

_____

_____

_____

_____

_____

_____

Personal promises to pray for your grandchildren:

_____

_____

_____

_____

_____

_____

_____

_____

_____

_____

_____

_____

Personal promises to pray for your grandchildren:

_____

_____

_____

_____

_____

_____

_____

_____

_____

_____

Personal promises to pray for your grandchildren:

_____

_____

_____

_____

_____

_____

_____

_____

_____

_____

_____

Let us ask for grace to
take up our place as priests with joy,
and give our life to bring down
the blessing of heaven.

ANDREW MURRAY

Journal of Prayers
Asked & Answered

Prayer _____

_____

_____

Answer_____

_____

_____

Prayer _____

_____

Answer_____

_____

_____

Prayer _____

_____

_____

Answer _____

_____

_____

Prayer _____

_____

_____

Answer_____

_____

_____

Prayer _____

_____

_____

Answer _____

_____

_____

Prayer _____

_____

_____

Answer _____

_____

_____

Prayer _____

_____

_____

Answer_____

_____

_____

Prayer _____

_____

_____

Answer_____

_____

_____

Prayer _____

_____

_____

Answer_____

_____

_____

Prayer _____

_____

Answer_____

_____

_____

Prayer _____

_____

_____

Answer _____

_____

_____

Prayer _____

_____

_____

Answer _____

_____

_____

Prayer _____

_____

_____

Answer _____

_____

_____

Prayer _____

_____

_____

Answer _____

_____

_____

Prayer _____

_____

_____

Answer _____

_____

_____

Prayer _____

_____

_____

Answer _____

_____

_____

Prayer _____

_____

_____

Answer _____

_____

_____

Prayer _____

_____

_____

Answer _____

_____

_____

Prayer _____

_____

_____

Answer _____

_____

_____

Prayer _____

_____

_____

Answer _____

_____

_____

Prayer _____
_____
_____

Answer _____
_____
_____

Prayer _____
_____

Answer _____
_____
_____